SHORT WALKS PEAK DISTRICT

BUXTON, DOVE DALE AND THE SOUTH WEST PEAK

by Andrew McCloy

The River Dove near Milldale (Walk 14)

CONTENTS

Using this guide. 4
Route summary table 6
Map key 7
Introduction. 9
  Walk in the South West Peak 10
  Where to stay. 11
  Getting around 11
  Caring for our national park. 11

The walks

1.	Danebridge and Lud's Church	13
2.	Taxal and Fernilee Reservoir	19
3.	Errwood Hall	25
4.	Three Shires Head	31
5.	The Roaches	37
6.	Buxton, Light Wood and Corbar Hill	43
7.	Buxton and Grin Low	49
8.	Hollinsclough and Chrome Hill	53
9.	Warslow and Revidge	59
10.	Wetton and Thor's Cave	65
11.	Hulme End and Ecton Hill	71
12.	Hartington and Beresford Dale	75
13.	Ilam and the Manifold valley	81
14.	Milldale and the River Dove	87
15.	Dove Dale	91

Useful information. 95

USING THIS GUIDE

Routes in this book

In this book you will find a selection of easy or moderate walks suitable for almost everyone, including casual walkers and families with children, or for when you only have a short time to fill. The routes have been carefully chosen to allow you to explore the area and its attractions. Most routes are circular or out-and-back, although some linear walks may be included that use public transport to get back to the start. Although there may be some climbs there is no challenging terrain, but do bear in mind that conditions can sometimes be wet or muddy underfoot. A route summary table is included on page 6 to help you choose the right walk.

Clothing and footwear

You won't need any special equipment to enjoy these walks. The weather in Britain can be changeable, so choose clothing suitable for the season and wear or carry a waterproof jacket. For footwear, comfortable walking boots or trainers with a good grip are best. A small rucksack for drinks, snacks and spare clothing is useful. See www.adventuresmart.uk.

Walk descriptions

At the beginning of each walk you'll find all the information you need:

- start/finish location, with a what3words address to help you find it
- parking and transport information, estimated walking time, total distance and climb
- details of public toilets available along the route and where you can get refreshments
- a summary of the key highlights of the walk and what you might see

Timings given are the time to complete the walk at a reasonable walking pace. Allow extra time for extended stops or if walking with children.

The route is described in clear, easy-to-follow directions, with each waypoint marked on an accompanying map extract. It's a good idea to read the whole of the route instructions before setting out, so that you know what to expect.

Maps, GPX files and what3words

Extracts from the OS® 1:25,000 map accompany each route. GPX files for all the walks in this book are available to download at www.cicerone.co.uk/1259/gpx.

What3words is a free smartphone app which identifies every 3m square of the globe with a unique three-word address, e.g. ///destiny.cafe.sonic. For more information see https://what3words.com/products/what3words-app.

USING THIS GUIDE

Walking with children

Even young children can be surprisingly strong walkers, but every family is different and you may need to adapt the timings given in this book to take that into account. Make sure you go at the pace of the slowest member and choose a walk with an exciting objective in mind, such as a cave, river, waterfall or picnic spot. Many of the walks can be shortened to suit – suggestions are included at the end of the route description.

Dogs

Sheep or cattle may be found grazing on a number of these walks. Keep dogs under control at all times so that they don't scare or disturb livestock or wildlife. Cattle, particularly cows with calves, may very occasionally pose a risk to walkers with dogs. If you ever feel threatened by cattle, you should let go of your dog's lead and let it run free.

Enjoying the countryside responsibly

Enjoy the countryside and treat it with respect to protect our natural environments. Stick to footpaths and take your litter home with you. When driving, slow down on rural roads and park considerately, or better still use public transport. For more details check out www.gov.uk/countryside-code.

The Countryside Code

Respect everyone
- be considerate to those living in, working in and enjoying the countryside
- leave gates and property as you find them
- do not block access to gateways or driveways when parking
- be nice, say hello, share the space
- follow local signs and keep to marked paths unless wider access is available

Protect the environment
- take your litter home – leave no trace of your visit
- do not light fires and only have BBQs where signs say you can
- always keep dogs under control and in sight
- dog poo – bag it and bin it – any public waste bin will do
- care for nature – do not cause damage or disturbance

Enjoy the outdoors
- check your route and local conditions
- plan your adventure – know what to expect and what you can do
- enjoy your visit, have fun, make a memory

ROUTE SUMMARY TABLE

WALK NAME	START POINT	TIME	DISTANCE
1. Danebridge and Lud's Church	Danebridge	2hr 30min	8km (5 miles)
2. Taxal and Fernilee Reservoir	A5004 layby near Whaley Bridge	3hr	10.2km (6.3 miles)
3. Errwood Hall	Errwood Hall car park	1hr 30min	4.3km (2.7 miles)
4. Three Shires Head	Gradbach car park	2hr	6.4km (4 miles)
5. The Roaches	Roaches Gate near Upper Hulme	2hr 15min	7.2km (4.5 miles)
6. Buxton, Light Wood and Corbar Hill	Buxton Opera House	2hr	6km (3.7 miles)
7. Buxton and Grin Low	Poole's Cavern, Buxton	1hr 15min	3.5km (2.2 miles)
8. Hollinsclough and Chrome Hill	Hollinsclough	2hr 30min	6.4km (4 miles)
9. Warslow and Revidge	Greyhound Inn, Warslow	1hr 45min	4.7km (2.9 miles)
10. Wetton and Thor's Cave	Wetton car park	2hr 30min	6.8km (4.2 miles)
11. Hulme End and Ecton Hill	Manifold Valley Visitor Centre	2hr	5.7km (3.5 miles)
12. Hartington and Beresford Dale	Market Place, Hartington	1hr 45min	6.6km (4.1 miles)
13. Ilam and the Manifold valley	Ilam Hall	2hr 45min	8.3km (5.2 miles)
14. Milldale and the River Dove	Milldale	1hr 30min	4.5km (2.8 miles)
15. Dove Dale	Dove Dale car park	2hr 45min	7.5km (4.7 miles)

ROUTE SUMMARY TABLE

HIGHLIGHTS
Riverside woodland, dramatic rock chasm
Peaceful river valley and scenic reservoir
Ruins of stately hall, views of moorland and reservoir
Historic bridge and packhorse routes
High rocky escarpment, climbing heritage, views
Nature reserve, hilltop views, spa town heritage
Woodland, country park and views over town
Exciting and undulating limestone ridge
Peaceful hilltop, birds and wildlife, views
Large cave, dramatic viewpoint high above valley
Mining heritage, hilltop views, former light railway
Attractive village and fishing river with literary association
Former mansion and elegant grounds, hilltop views, riverside
Wildlife-rich dale, hilltop views and scenic riverside path
Dramatic limestone scenery, riverside path and stepping stones

SYMBOLS USED ON ROUTE MAPS

- (S) Start point
- (F) Finish point
- (SF) Start and finish at the same place
- 4→ Waypoint
- ～ Route line

MAPPING IS SHOWN AT A SCALE OF 1:25,000

0 KM — 0.25 — 0.5
0 miles — 0.25

DOWNLOAD THE GPX FILES FOR FREE AT
www.cicerone.co.uk/1259/gpx

The high track to Hartington

INTRODUCTION

The Crescent in Buxton

The Peak District is a place of immense variety and contrast, and nowhere is that more evident than in its south west corner where the choice and quality of walking experiences is hard to beat. Here you will find spectacular limestone dales with angular hills and sparkling rivers, rugged open moorland giving way to scenic tree-lined reservoirs, plus an elegant spa town to rival any in the country. There are walking routes here for all tastes, all abilities and all weathers.

Dominating the skyline of what's often referred to as the South West Peak is a broad belt of high moorland, interspersed with gritstone outcrops, that stretches from Whaley Bridge in the north all the way south to Leek and defines the national park's western edge. Rivers and reservoirs are spawned on these high slopes, many of which provide excellent walking routes for this book. To the east sits historic Buxton, England's highest market town and one which has been attracting visitors since the Romans discovered its thermal spa waters. Different again are the narrow and partly wooded limestone valleys of the rivers Dove and Manifold that flow south towards Ashbourne, rich in wildlife and dramatic landscape features, and whose riverside paths offer more delectable walks.

Chrome Hill from Hollinsclough (Walk 8)

Walk in the South West Peak

The walks in this book are circular and all involve some measure of up and down – this is the Peak District, after all. They range from leisurely outings around the attractive reservoirs of Errwood and Fernilee in the Goyt valley, or a short circuit of Buxton's leafy country park, through to more adventurous and undulating routes exploring Dove Dale and the Manifold valley. Some of these involve steeper slopes or steps and may be rough underfoot in places, but the paths are generally well waymarked and maintained.

There are stories and surprises waiting for you on every walk. Sometimes it's a jaw-dropping natural feature like the rock chasm of Lud's Church, hidden deep in the woods above Danebridge, or the scaly 'dragon's back' ridge of Chrome Hill in the upper Dove valley. For airy drama head for the Roaches, a line of staccato gritstone outcrops that puncture the Staffordshire skyline; or stand on Corbar Hill for a sensational view across Buxton's rooftops. Elsewhere, the pleasures are more subtle and sensuous, like the stepping stone crossing of the River Dove; or listening to the skylarks and curlews on the peaceful heather moors of Revidge above Warslow.

This is also a place where people have left their mark, from the Bronze

Age bones found in Thor's Cave high above the Manifold valley through to the ancient packhorse bridge and historic trading routes at Three Shires Head. Ecton Hill once echoed to the sounds of a busy copper mine; the River Dove near Hartington inspired a book on fly fishing that became an unlikely and enduring bestseller; while the walks at Ilam and Errwood hark back to a Victorian era of opulent stately homes.

Where to stay

The obvious base for exploring the area is Buxton, which has plenty of accommodation, shops and places to eat. Ashbourne and Leek are handily placed on the southern edge and attractive towns in their own right, while Whaley Bridge is an option to the north. Villages like Hartington, Wetton, Warslow, Longnor and Thorpe all have pubs and in some instances cafes and shops. Many have self-catering accommodation and a few (like Hulme End) have campsites; and you can even stay quite cheaply in grand period buildings – the Grade II listed Ilam Hall and Hartington Hall youth hostels!

Getting around

Buxton is the main hub for public transport connections. There are daily services from surrounding places like Stockport, Macclesfield, Stoke and Sheffield, as well as more locally from towns like Bakewell and Leek. It also has a direct railway link to Manchester, around one hour's travel time. Village buses are more infrequent, but in rural Staffordshire the Moorlands Connect service operates on-demand minibuses for communities and visitors across the Staffordshire moorlands – you simply book your ride in advance.

Caring for our national park

The Peak District National Park covers 1438km^2 (555 miles^2) and for 70 years it has been a firm favourite with walkers, but although places like Dove Dale can get busy you don't have to walk far to get away from the crowds and enjoy peace and quiet.

Indeed, exploring on foot is not just one of the most rewarding ways to discover the Peak District, it's also the most sustainable. The national park is a precious but fragile environment, where there's a delicate balance between recreation, conservation and the day-to-day life of farming communities, so enjoy this glorious landscape – but tread lightly. To put something back please support the work of the Peak District National Park Foundation, a charity set up to raise funds to care for the national park (www.peakdistrictfoundation.org.uk).

Mature oak on the valley path

WALK 1
Danebridge and Lud's Church

Start/finish	Danebridge
Locate	///craftsmen.juniors.video
Cafes/pubs	Brewery in Danebridge
Transport	Moorlands Connect bus
Parking	Roadside at Danebridge, near Wincle (SK11 0QE)
Toilets	No public toilets on route

Time 2hr 30min
Distance 8km (5 miles)
Climb 205m

Uncover a mysterious legend and natural wonder deep in the woods on this adventurous outing

From ancient woodland and a spectacular rock chasm to an open escarpment with stupendous views, this energetic and absorbing walk with plenty of ups and downs has it all. Follow an Arthurian tale of knights in deadly combat to the secretive chasm known as Lud's Church deep in the woods. And what better way to relax when it's all done than with some locally prepared refreshment at the inviting Wincle Brewery?

Wincle Brewery at Danebridge clearly welcomes walkers!

1 On the southern (Staffordshire) side of the high-arched road bridge over the River Dane take the footpath signposted Gradbach via Dane valley. The Grade II listed road bridge soaring above the river was built in 1869 to replace a lower bridge a little way downstream. Follow this obvious route up the valley, at first beside the river then higher up through trees, for 1.2km until you reach the buildings of **Back Dane**.

Dane bridge

Across much of the South West Peak the traditional building stone is gritstone, in various hues of grey, but around Danebridge and Wincle you'll see evidence of the local sandstone. It's a soft yellow or reddish-buff colour, often accompanied by Kerridge stone slate roofs instead of Staffordshire blue tiles.

2 Follow the surfaced driveway for a few paces, then continue on the waymarked route across open hillside past **Back Forest Farm** into woods. After 2km join another track and go downhill as far as a giant old beech tree at a junction of routes just above the river.

The glorious broadleaved woodland beside the river contains oak, birch, alder and rowan, with

WALK 1 – DANEBRIDGE AND LUD'S CHURCH

a carpet of wildflowers including wood anemone, native bluebell, yellow archangel and wood sorrel. Such a diverse mix indicates that this is likely to be a remnant of ancient woodland (woods that have existed since AD1600).

> ⓘ *A silk cloth called Leek Raven made with black dye from coal dust at a mill in Danebridge was popularised by Queen Victoria in mourning.*

3 Go right, up some stone steps, and right again on a broad uphill track signposted Lud's Church until you reach a small clearing by a rocky outcrop.

4 Turn left at the path junction and after 200m go right into the narrow rocky entrance to **Lud's Church**.

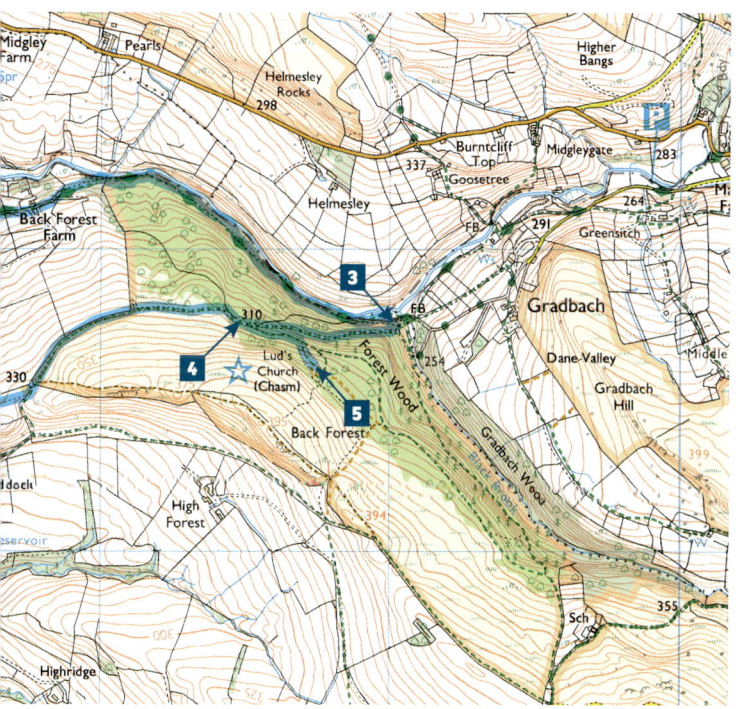

5 When you've finished exploring retrace your steps to Waypoint 4, then go straight on, gently uphill and out across open hillside. Continue ahead at the next path junction, signposted Swythamley, then 100m further on take the concessionary path on the right, via a high wall stile. Walk across the hilltop to a gritstone outcrop known as **Hanging Stone**. From the top there are panoramic views of the nearby peak of Shutlingsloe and the Roaches, as well as further afield across the Cheshire Plain.

6 Follow the path down below the rocky outcrop to the track at the bottom. Turn right, then just past **Hangingstone Farm** take the signposted path on the left slanting down through two fields. Continue down a small valley newly planted with trees to reach the track at the bottom. Turn left to return to the start.

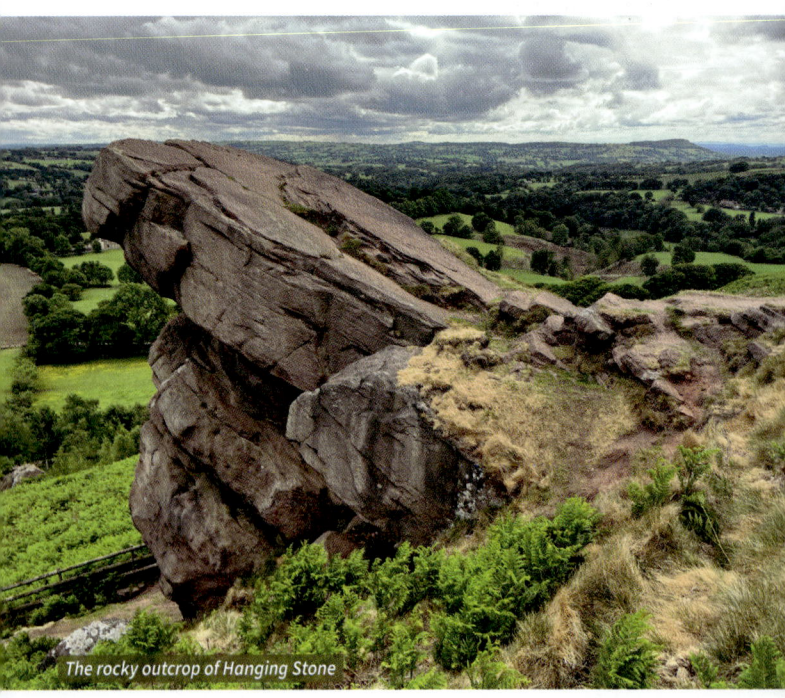
The rocky outcrop of Hanging Stone

Wincle Brewery, seen from the bridge at the start of the walk, produces a range of high-quality traditional ales. Their welcoming 'Sampling Room' has indoor and outdoor seating and is open daily, with non-alcoholic and hot drinks also available.

Myth and legend at Lud's Church

Mosses and ferns abound in the cool damp atmosphere of Lud's Church

Originally caused by a landslip, Lud's Church is a deep natural chasm in the rocks whose steep rocky sides are covered in ferns, mosses and lichens thanks to the permanently cool, damp atmosphere. It's well concealed by woodland and over the years has been a place of refuge and secretive worship. However, some also believe it to be the setting of a 14th-century poem in which Sir Gawain, a knight of the Round Table, vanquishes the rebellious Green Knight in a mysterious and supernatural 'Green Chapel' deep in the rocks. If ever there was a place for Arthurian myth and legend this must surely be it!

Footbridge over the River Goyt to Hillbridge and Park Wood

WALK 2
Taxal and Fernilee Reservoir

Time 3hr
Distance 10.2km (6.3 miles)
Climb 180m

Trace the River Goyt and its changing valley landscape on a long but quite easy walk

Start/finish	Layby off A5004 Buxton Road, near Whaley Bridge
Locate	///frown.stole.seasick
Cafes/pubs	None on route
Transport	Buses from Buxton, Whaley Bridge and New Mills
Parking	Layby off A5004 Buxton Road (SK23 7DY)
Toilets	No public toilets on route

This walk begins and ends near the hamlet of Taxal, south of Whaley Bridge, where the unfettered young River Goyt flows through wildlife-rich meadows and woods. Further upstream you see how the valley has been altered to form Fernilee Reservoir, with a walking route around its tree-lined shores that is scenic and relaxing. Although quite long, this is an uncomplicated route that's easy to follow and for much of the way almost level.

Taxal church

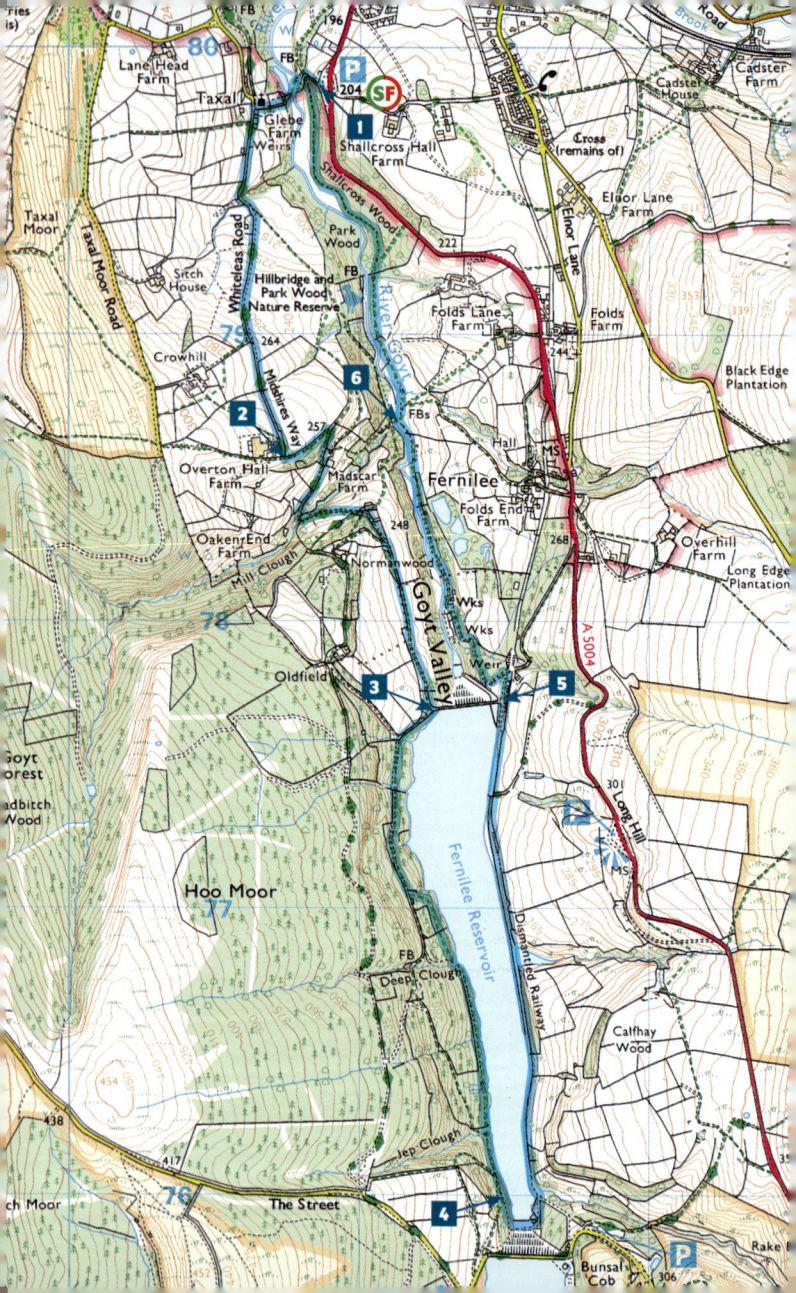

WALK 2 – TAXAL AND FERNILEE RESERVOIR

View from the path above the reservoir's western shore

1 From the layby walk down the steep track to cross the footbridge over the River Goyt. Follow it back up to a junction by the Church of St James at **Taxal**. Although medieval in origin, the church was largely rebuilt in the 1800s in the simple Gothic style of the day. Turn left and walk along the lane, which becomes an unsurfaced and gently rising farm track across fields to **Overton Hall Farm**.

2 Turn left at the junction and follow the wide track downhill past **Madscar Farm**, then up the other side of the valley via Knipe Farm. Stay on this gated route until you reach **Fernilee Reservoir**.

A little further down the valley, near Whaley Bridge, is Toddbrook Reservoir. In 2019 flood damage to the reservoir wall led to fears of a total collapse and the town's 6500 population was evacuated. After draining, the dam was repaired and the reservoir has slowly refilled.

3 Keep the dam on your left and walk straight on along a track, then turn left on a path signposted Errwood through the semi-wooded hillside. After 550m turn left down a stepped path to the wooded shoreline and follow this route all the way to a path junction at the far end of the reservoir.

Fernilee Reservoir dam

Errwood Reservoir has a capacity of around 5 billion litres and is connected to the smaller Fernilee Reservoir by underground tunnels.

4 Turn left down steps and across the open area below the huge grass-topped dam of **Errwood Reservoir**. On the far side swing left down a gravel track and then driveway to walk along a straight flat track beside Fernilee Reservoir for 1.8km until you reach the dam.

5 Walk past (not over) the dam and continue ahead along the road. Go left at the bend down a private road (also a public footpath). Continue beyond the waterworks buildings and out across fields next to the **River Goyt** until you reach a footbridge.

> ⓘ *The emblem of Staffordshire, widely used throughout the county, is the distinctive three-looped Staffordshire knot.*

WALK 2 – TAXAL AND FERNILEE RESERVOIR

To visit Hillbridge and Park Wood nature reserve cross the footbridge. In spring this extensive oak woodland beside the river, managed by Derbyshire Wildlife Trust, is carpeted by bluebells and alive with the sound of birds like warblers and chiffchaffs, while dippers and kingfishers can be seen in the river.

6 Continue on the path downstream with the river on your left. Walk through **Shallcross Wood** and at the junction at the far end turn right along the track to walk back up to the start.

− To shorten
At Waypoint 3 turn left on to the lane and walk across the dam, resuming the route at Waypoint 5. This saves 4km and about 1hr.

From the moors to the Mersey

The River Goyt rises on Axe Edge Moor, south west of Buxton, and flows for 49km via New Mills to join the River Tame at Stockport, where it forms the River Mersey. It was the growing demand for water from the downstream urban population that led Stockport Corporation to construct Fernilee Reservoir in the 1930s, with Errwood following in the 1960s. Before this the upper Goyt valley was a pastoral landscape of scattered woods and farms, but it was by no means undeveloped. As well as notable buildings like Errwood Hall (see Walk 3), there was a large gunpowder factory here and even a railway along what is now the reservoir's eastern shore.

Former Stockport Corporation Water Works sign beside the path

Rhododendrons near Errwood Hall

WALK 3
Errwood Hall

Start/finish	*Errwood Hall car park*
Locate	*///saying.suffix.engulfing*
Cafes/pubs	*None on route*
Transport	*No public transport*
Parking	*Errwood Hall car park (SK17 6GJ)*
Toilets	*No public toilets on route*

Today the upper Goyt valley is largely unpopulated, its reservoirs attractively fringed by woods and open moorland and a popular place for recreation; but once it contained a stylish and opulent mansion that served as a busy family home. This short walk, which includes a long but steady ascent of an open ridge above the trees, takes you to the remains of Errwood Hall and a glimpse of a life long gone.

Time 1hr 30min
Distance 4.3km (2.7 miles)
Climb 175m

A short walk around a quiet valley near Buxton that reveals the story of a long-lost family mansion

The gentle ascent of Foxlow Edge

1 From the back of the car park follow waymarks for Errwood Hall woodland walk past the noticeboard and across an open area. Beyond a wall gap go straight on and down into a lush, wooded ravine. The Grimshaws of Errwood Hall introduced exotic plants like rhododendrons and azaleas that they brought back from their overseas travels, and these continue to thrive today. Follow the track as it begins to climb and at a junction double back sharply to the right to reach the ruins of **Errwood Hall**.

The few surviving photos of Errwood Hall show an impressive double-winged, turreted building, including a private Catholic chapel, while outside were ornamental gardens, pathways and elaborate fountains. For images and information see www.goyt-valley.org.uk.

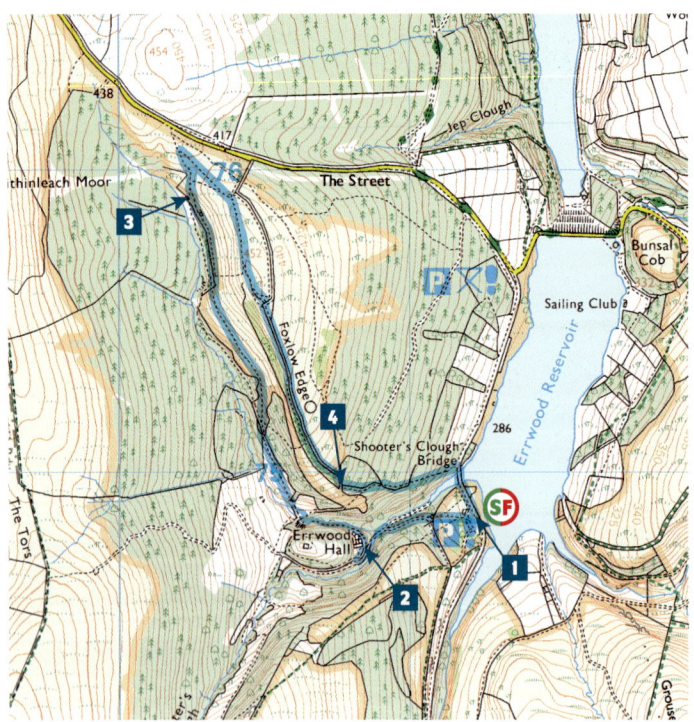

WALK 3 – ERRWOOD HALL

Little is left of Errwood Hall today

2 Continue along the path past the remains of the hall and go down to cross a small stream via rough stepping stones. At a junction go right, up a short flight of steps. Turn left on a path past a bench. Continue steadily up the part-wooded valley, going straight on at a junction for 1.2km to reach a small circular stone building on your left.

This is St Joseph's Shrine, also known as the Spanish Shrine. It was built by the Grimshaw family to honour Spanish-born Sister Dolores, who set up the school at the hall and after Samuel Grimshaw's death in 1883 became his widow's companion.

Interior of St Joseph's Shrine

St Joseph's Shrine, also known as the Spanish Shrine

3 Continue up the path for around 200m, then just before the road turn right at a path junction. Follow the route along the open top of **Foxlow Edge** until you start to drop gradually downhill. Keep the wall on your right and descend until you reach the corner of a fenced plantation. Among the buildings cleared in the 1930s to make way for the new reservoir was Errwood Hall Farm, which briefly served as a youth hostel.

4 Stay on the main path as it swings left, beside the fence. Go straight on at another junction and all the way down to **Shooters Clough Bridge**. Turn right and walk across the bridge and along the road the short distance to the car park.

On most weekends of the year the reservoir is used by Errwood Sailing Club for sailing and windsurfing. They have a clubhouse, slipways and pontoon on the far side of the water and hold regular events and competitions.

> ⓘ *There are 62 reservoirs of various sizes within the Peak District National Park, but no natural lakes.*

The former splendour of Errwood Hall

In 1840 Samuel Grimshaw, a wealthy merchant from Manchester, chose the remote upper Goyt valley as the place to build a grand country house. It was designed in the style of an Italian villa, complete with a small school, stables and formal gardens, and for almost a century served as the family home. However, when the last of the Grimshaw line died in 1930 the hall and estate were purchased by Stockport Corporation, who then demolished the buildings as part of their plans to clear the valley and construct Fernilee Reservoir (see Walk 2). Today only the foundations and a few surviving walls from the mansion remain as a forlorn reminder of its former glories.

On top of Foxlow Edge

Taking the plunge in Panniers Pool

WALK 4
Three Shires Head

Start/finish	*Gradbach car park*
Locate	*///develop.entitles.bonus*
Cafes/pubs	*Seasonal weekend cafe at Gradbach Mill (500m off route)*
Transport	*Moorlands Connect bus*
Parking	*Gradbach car park (SK17 0SU)*
Toilets	*No public toilets on route*

Time 2hr
Distance 6.4km (4 miles)
Climb 150m

Follow field and moorland tracks across county borders tracing historic packhorse routes beside the River Dane

This may be an uncomplicated walk in the open Dane valley across rough fields and moorland tracks, but you end up visiting three separate counties, as well as an area once notorious for its lawlessness. The highlight of the walk is a picturesque packhorse bridge sitting in a cleft of the moors above the tumbling river and its cool dark pools – a perfect place for a paddle on a hot sunny day.

Path along the Dane Valley

SHORT WALKS PEAK DISTRICT

1 Take the path from Staffordshire Wildlife Trust's free car park beside the **River Dane** and head upstream to cross a footbridge. Walk along the open riverbank and up to a gate onto the lane. Turn right and after the sharp bend go left by Dane View House. Just along the lane from the car park at the start is the Coffee Cabin at Gradbach Mill, serving light refreshments from Easter to October.

2 Go through a gate and ahead across fields, close to a wall on your left. Carry straight on when the wall ends and cross an area of rougher ground to reach a signpost.

The remote area around Three Shires Head was once the scene of illegal pursuits such as cock fighting and bare-knuckle fighting, aided by the fact that the miscreants could evade arrest by the police of one county by simply hopping across the border and out of their jurisdiction.

3 Turn left, signed to Three Shires Head, for a grassy track via a gate which swings around the hillside. Join a farm track, then after 120m go right at a signpost for a path that slants up the hillside to join a track at the top. Turn left and follow this to the

The packhorse bridge at Three Shires Head

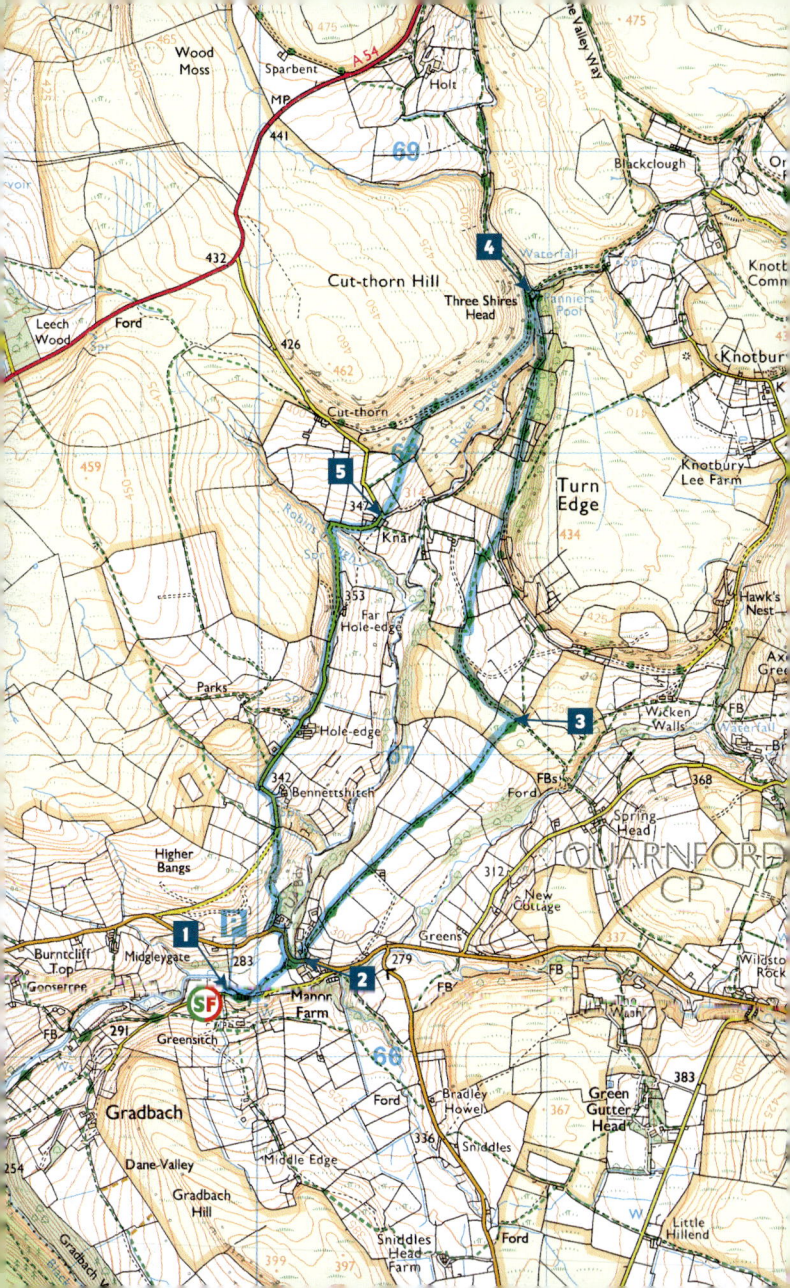

A quiet lane in the Dane valley

packhorse bridge over the River Dane at **Three Shires Head**.

> The River Dane marks the boundary between Staffordshire (on the east bank) and Cheshire (west bank), but just before you step onto the old packhorse bridge you are momentarily in Derbyshire – making three counties in a single walk!

4 Go over the narrow bridge and turn left. Follow the wide track high above the river for 550m and go left at a waymark. Follow the path through a wall gate and across fields to reach **Knar Farm** and go up to the lane above.

> Beside the lane you may notice a Coal Authority sign, since nearby is the former Danebower Colliery. It was worked until 1925 and was one of over 50 small coal mines that were once active in the South West Peak.

5 Follow this little-used gated lane for 1.3km then, just after **Bennettshitch Farm**, take the path on the left down the scrubby hillside to

WALK 4 – THREE SHIRES HEAD

reach the road at the bottom. Turn left, over the bridge by the chapel. Above the chapel door you can just make out a faded sign that says 'Registered for the Solemnization of Marriages'. Pass back into Staffordshire from Cheshire, then take the path on the right to return along the riverside to the start.

Packhorse routes of the Peak District

The attractive stone bridge at Three Shires Head was built to accommodate packhorses, its parapets deliberately low to allow clearance for the ponies' loads (and beneath the bridge is so-called Panniers Pool). Several different packhorse routes converged on this location, with commodities like salt, cloth and corn coming one way and lead ore, charcoal and lime heading the other way. Packhorse trains of up to 25 or 30 tough and sure-footed little ponies were a familiar sight in the Peak District from medieval times until the 1750s. Indeed, for a long period they were the only way to transport goods across the remote hills.

Wesleyan chapel near Gradbach

Climbers on the Roaches

WALK 5
The Roaches

Start/finish	*Roaches Gate, Roach Road, near Upper Hulme*
Locate	*///crashing.flamingo.released*
Cafes/pubs	*Tea room 1km from start*
Transport	*Moorlands Connect bus*
Parking	*Roadside in marked bays only (ST13 8TY)*
Toilets	*No public toilets on route*

Time 2hr 15min
Distance 7.2km (4.5 miles)
Climb 215m

Enjoy panoramic views from a striking gritstone edge on this straightforward circuit

Guarding the south west entrance to the Peak District like a row of artillery guns, the craggy gritstone edges known as the Roaches offer spectacular views and a comparatively level path that runs almost all the way along the top. It's a little rough underfoot in places and there are some steep stone steps at one point, otherwise this airy loop through the Staffordshire moorlands is easy to follow, with views as far as North Wales on a clear day.

Doxey Pool

The path to Hen Cloud

1 Go through the roadside gate and walk up the main track, ignoring a left turn. Go through another gate and continue as far as a junction of routes, with the prominent summit of **Hen Cloud** to your right. To the south west is Tittesworth Reservoir, from where Severn Trent pump over 28 million litres of water daily to the towns of Leek and Stoke-on-Trent.

The Roaches are managed by Staffordshire Wildlife Trust who took on the long-term lease of this iconic estate from the National Park Authority in 2013. Since then they have improved paths, rebuilt walls and restored wildlife-rich blanket bog vital for storing carbon.

2 Go straight on, signposted Upper Hulme, and stay on the track across undulating ground of heather and bracken. At a gate join a vehicle track and continue ahead. Immediately after the next gate turn left for a grassy path beside a fence. Pass to the right of **Shawtop Farm** and join its driveway until you reach a lane.

3 Turn left and follow the open moorland lane for 2km until you reach the tight bend at **Roach End**, at the northern end of the ridge.

WALK 5 – THE ROACHES

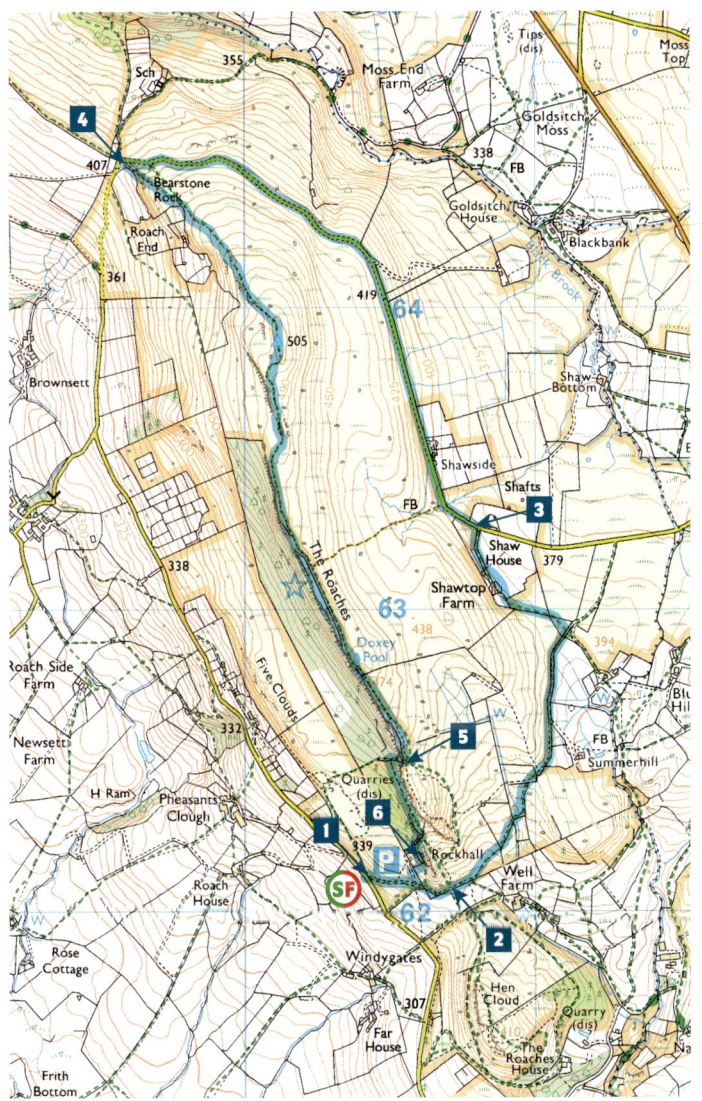

39

4 Turn left up a stepped path, opposite the drive to Roach End Farm. Follow this partly paved and obvious route along the top of **the Roaches**. Go past a trig point, and further on **Doxey Pool**, and reach a junction of paths. The dark peaty waters of Doxey Pool are supposedly home to a malevolent mermaid called Jenny Greenteeth, who lures passers-by to a watery grave. Be warned!

For many years the moorlands surrounding the Roaches were home to a small but unlikely colony of red-necked wallabies. They escaped from a private zoo in the 1930s and would occasionally pop up to startle passing ramblers.

ⓘ *The Roaches take their name from the French word* rochers *meaning rocks.*

5 Turn right for a path down between a gap in the rocks and at the bottom turn left at a junction. Follow the route through trees at the foot of the rock face. Go right, down steep stone steps, and then left to reach **Rockhall** cottage, also known as the Don Whillans Memorial Hut.

6 Walk past the front of the building, go over a stile and fork right down a path. Go left at the bottom, then right to rejoin the main track to the start.

Walking along the Roaches

WALK 5 – THE ROACHES

Rockhall cottage partly carved out of rock

✚ To lengthen

For a there-and-back ascent of Hen Cloud leave the main route at Waypoint 2 and follow the obvious track straight ahead to the summit, a round journey of 1.2km (40min) involving 70m of ascent.

A rock dwelling under the Roaches

Rockhall is a remarkable stone dwelling partly carved out of the rock itself. It was built in 1862 as a gamekeeper's cottage and, despite not having mains water or electricity, was inhabited until as late as 1990. Today it's owned by the British Mountaineering Council (BMC) and used by climbers. The building is also known as the Don Whillans Memorial Hut in honour of the legendary mountaineer from Manchester who first met his equally famous climbing partner Joe Brown on the Roaches in 1951.

Corbar Hill cross with Buxton's rooftops beyond

WALK 6
Buxton, Light Wood and Corbar Hill

Start/finish	*Buxton Opera House*
Locate	*///cabinets.objecting.moving*
Cafes/pubs	*Options at Pavilion, cafe and pubs in town centre*
Transport	*Wide range of bus services. Trains from Manchester*
Parking	*Pavilion Gardens, St John's Road, Buxton (SK17 9AR)*
Toilets	*At Pavilion and town centre*

This walk begins and ends in Buxton's elegant town centre and traces its origins as a fashionable spa resort. In between it explores a little-visited nature reserve and culminates in a hilltop vantage point high above the rooftops. The route combines urban streets and parks with some rougher paths and a sharp climb, as well as a short section of open moorland that may be boggy after wet weather.

Time 2hr
Distance 6km (3.7 miles)
Climb 175m

Discover Buxton's spa heritage on this varied and undulating town and countryside route

The Octagon with Derbyshire's county flag

SHORT WALKS PEAK DISTRICT

1 From the Opera House entrance walk up Water Street. At the top turn right to cross the A53 at the roundabout. Go up Devonshire Road, past the Devonshire Dome. This extraordinary building has an unsupported dome that is larger than those of St Paul's Cathedral or the Pantheon in Rome. Go right into Marlborough Road, right again into Corbar Road and at the end turn left into Lightwood Road and continue straight on after the houses end to reach **Light Wood**.

This tucked-away valley off the tourist trail once contained two small reservoirs that supplied Buxton with drinking water, but now it's managed as a nature reserve by Derbyshire Wildlife Trust and the woods, wetland and moors support an abundance of wildlife.

2 Go past utility buildings on a rising path. Ignore a right turn and follow the main path as it swings right beside a watercourse. At the far end go right, up steps, then left over a small footbridge. Go left and cross another. Turn right to climb a steep winding path. At the top turn left on a path close to a wall to reach the far top corner.

3 Cross the fence stile on the right and out onto open moorland. Turn left and follow a rough path for 180m. Climb the fence stile on your left and walk across the open hilltop pasture, close to a wall on your left, to

Light Wood valley

WALK 6 – BUXTON, LIGHT WOOD AND CORBAR HILL

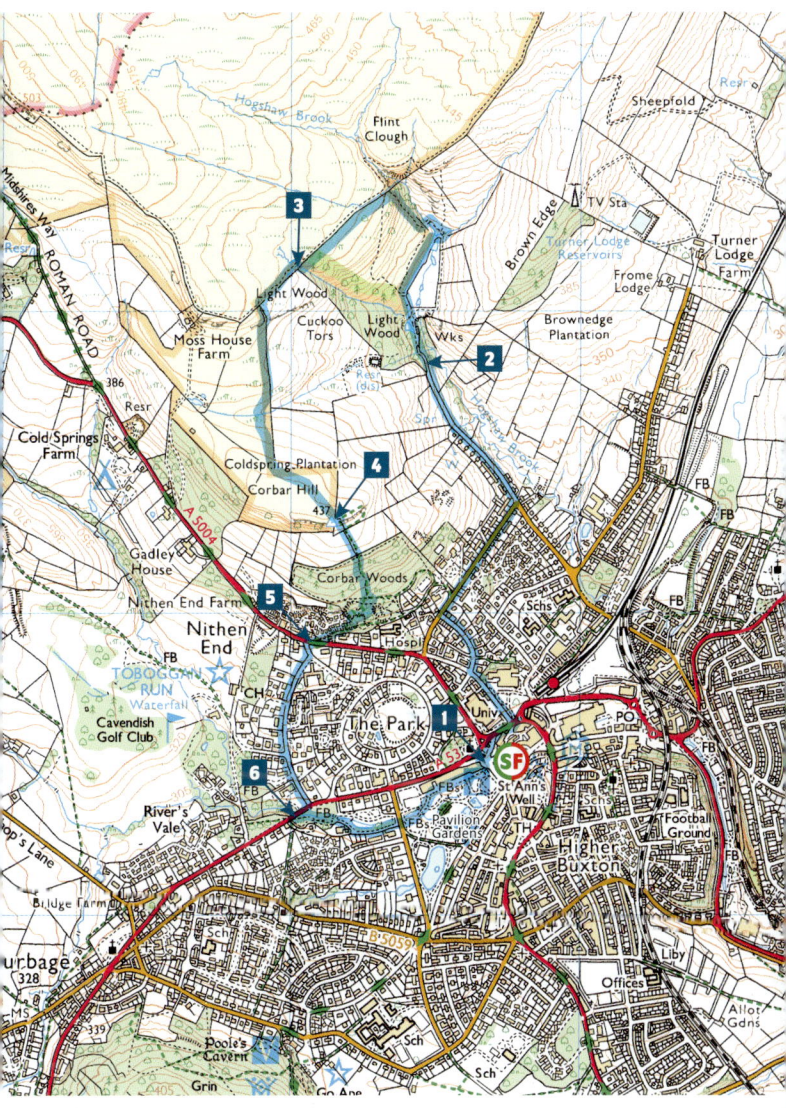

45

The moorland path to Corbar Hill

Corbar Hill topped by a large cross. The prominent wooden cross was erected by Buxton's Catholic community in 1950 to celebrate the Jubilee or Holy Year.

4 At the summit go through the gate on the left and then turn right on the path down through the rocks to **Corbar Woods**.

Corbar Woods is Buxton's only surviving semi-natural woodland, partly evidenced by a large area of bluebells in spring. It also contains a network of landscaped paths created as fashionable woodland walks during the Victorian era.

Descend ahead through the trees until you come to a cross-path by a clearing and woodland activity area. Turn right and then left to follow the gently winding main path downhill to the road below.

5 Cross over Manchester Road, turn right then left into Park Road. Go right into Carlisle Road and at the very bottom cross over St John's Road and

> ⓘ *As well as the renowned Buxton International arts festival, the town also hosts the annual Festival Fringe and the long-running Gilbert and Sullivan Festival.*

turn right. Immediately after the bridge turn left into Serpentine Walks.

Buxton Opera House

6 Follow the path beside the River Wye and at the end cross Burlington Road and continue opposite through Pavilion Gardens. Walk past the Octagon, bandstand and Conservatory to return to the Opera House at the far end. Buxton Opera House was designed by Frank Matcham in 1903 and this grand Edwardian edifice remains a popular venue for concerts and shows.

– To shorten

Emerging from the woods at Waypoint 5, turn left and walk down Manchester Road back to the town centre, saving 0.5km or 15min.

Taking the waters at Buxton

Buxton's geothermal springs first attracted the Romans, who named it Aquae Arnemetiae. Since then people have been coming to bathe in its mineral-rich waters and, of course, to drink the stuff, either free from the source at St Ann's Well or buying the well-known bottled product. The town's modern spa boom gave rise to some outstanding period architecture and public spaces, including The Crescent, a Grade I listed Georgian structure near the start of the walk, which was built as a centrepiece of the fashionable new spa town and restored in 2020. Also pause and admire the Octagon, part of the elegant Pavilion Gardens beside the Opera House.

Solomon's Temple or Grinlow Tower

WALK 7
Buxton and Grin Low

Start/finish	*Poole's Cavern, Buxton*
Locate	*///clockwork.unzipped.tungsten*
Cafes/pubs	*Cafe at Poole's Cavern*
Transport	*Wide range of bus services. Trains from Manchester*
Parking	*Poole's Cavern, Green Lane, Buxton (SK17 9DH)*
Toilets	*At Poole's Cavern*

Time 1hr 15min
Distance 3.5km (2.2 miles)
Climb 110m

A straightforward short walk through woodland up to a hilltop viewpoint associated with Buxton's industrial past

Despite Buxton's tourist appeal, many years ago the town's southern fringe was tainted by lime production, with quarries, smoking kilns and huge piles of waste material. Over a century later and the former industrial landscape of Grin Low is now a scenic country park, with open slopes and attractive broadleaved woodland. This short and fairly easy walk, with a long but gentle climb up through woods to a hilltop folly, rewards you with fabulous views over both the town and the wider Peak District.

The entrance to Poole's Cavern

1 From the car park at **Poole's Cavern** walk up the stepped path into the woods. Poole's Cavern is a large natural cave system and there are guided tours to see spectacular stalactites and stalagmites. Cross the main track and take the path uphill through Grin Woods, following regular blue waymark posts all the way. Go left at the top of the path, then fork right and up steps. At a junction go right, along the top of the edge of the wood, until you reach some steps on the left.

> ⓘ *Buxton is reputedly the highest town in England at over 300m above sea level and the nearby village of Flash is the highest village (463m).*

Poole's Cavern and its adjacent woodland is owned and managed by Buxton Civic Association, a charity set up to conserve and promote the town's natural and cultural heritage. Their excellent booklet guide to a circular woodland walk around Buxton called 'Ring of Trees' is available locally or via www.buxtoncivicassociation.org.uk.

2 Go up the steps, through a gate and ahead across the open grassy hilltop. Swing left and walk along the upper edge of the former quarry, now occupied by **Buxton Caravan Park**. Go across (not down) its entrance road and continue ahead, staying close to the fence on your left. Swing downhill to reach a gate.

Buxton and its quarries were kept outside the Peak District National Park boundary when it was drawn up in 1951 because of landscape impact and planning issues. Today major quarrying and lime production still takes place at nearby Tunstead and Hindlow.

Grin Woods

3 Go through the gate, along a fenced path past a junction, to the very far end. Turn right through a gate and out onto the open bumpy slope. Walk up to **Solomon's Temple** (also known as Grinlow Tower). The hilltop folly was built in 1869 by public subscription and is named after local landowner Solomon Mycock.

The bumpy summit of Grin Low reflects its industrial past

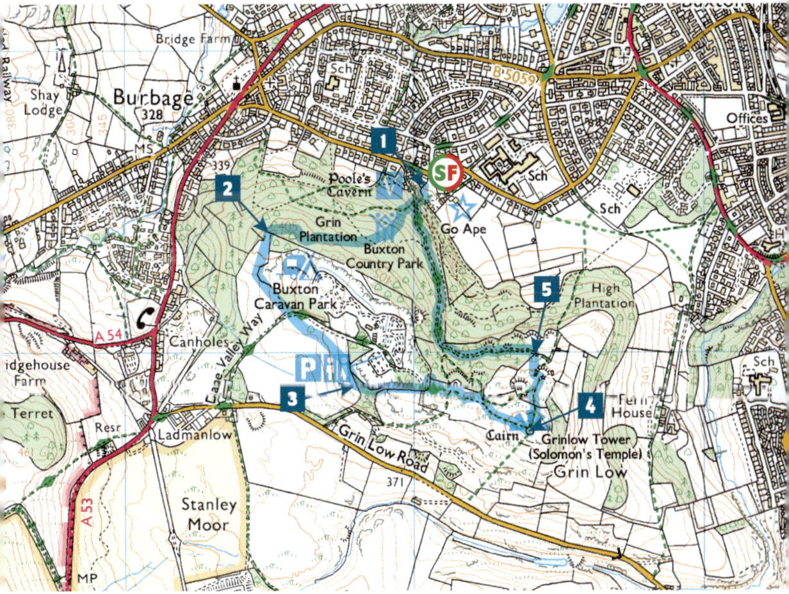

51

4 Leave the tower and descend the hillside northwards, with Buxton town centre directly below. Go through a wall gap and continue downhill, veering left to reach a gate and stile and re-enter the woods.

Grin Woods were planted from the 1820s onwards to provide the town with a green buffer from its lime-burning hinterland. The 40ha of beech, hazel, sycamore, birch and yew are among the highest broadleaved woods in the UK, at over 425m above sea level.

5 Follow the level track. At a junction at the far end turn right to join a wider route gently downhill and walk back to the car park at the start.

From industrial wasteland to country park

Buxton's lime industry flourished throughout the Industrial Revolution and involved the burning of locally quarried limestone to produce lime, which was used by farmers as fertiliser and by the building industry as mortar. As a result the town's southern landscape became pockmarked with quarries and a growing number of lime and coal spoil heaps, while the air was filled with smoke from dozens of kilns. Over a century of natural recovery later and the grassed-over hilltop is home to lime-loving plants like orchids and mountain pansy, with the mature woodland a Site of Special Scientific Interest and full of birdlife.

A life-size wooden sculpture of a lime worker

WALK 8
Hollinsclough and Chrome Hill

Start/finish	Hollinsclough
Locate	///graph.irrigate.dripped
Cafes/pubs	Seasonal weekend cafe at Hollinsclough
Transport	Moorlands Connect bus
Parking	Roadside in Hollinsclough (SK17 0RH)
Toilets	No public toilets on route

Time 2hr 30min
Distance 6.4km (4 miles)
Climb 235m

Scale the Dragon's Back on this undulating and exhilarating hill walk in the upper Dove valley

Chrome Hill is a relatively small but very prominent and angular hill, formed from a coral reef millions of years ago, that rises spectacularly above the infant River Dove near Longnor. This walk follows the popular route along the jagged ridge to the top for outstanding views. Although the path is well walked, it is steep and rocky in places with long drops and care should be taken, especially if the grassy slopes are slippery after rain.

Chrome Hill is known as the 'Dragon's Back'

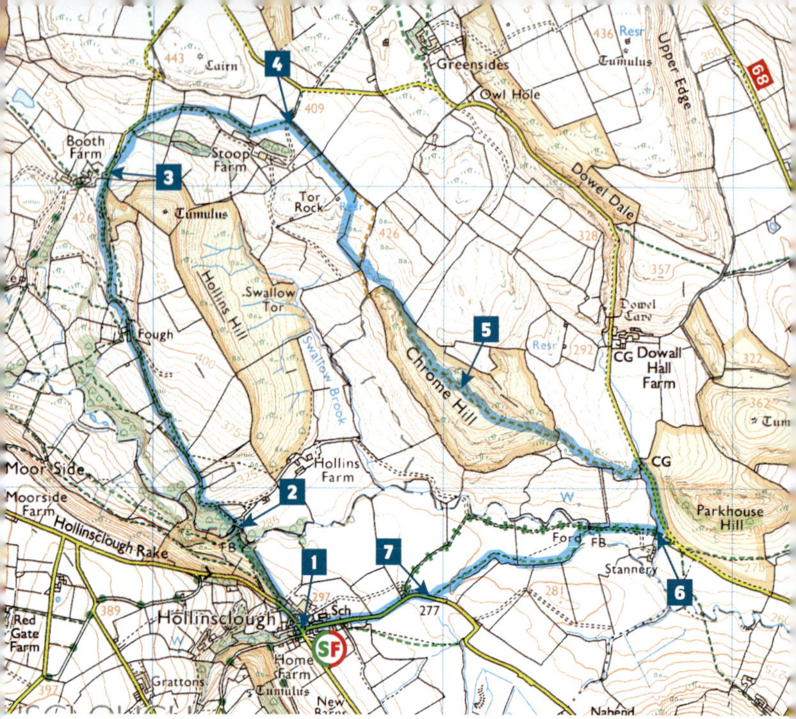

1 From the junction in the centre of **Hollinsclough** walk up the lane past the Methodist Chapel for 120m. Take the path on the right and follow this down the field with a wall to your right. At the bottom cross a footbridge and go up and through a gate.

The peaceful village of Hollinsclough

> In the 1700s many Hollinsclough families earned a living using hand looms to weave small silk items. The finished articles were then transported over the moors by packhorse to Macclesfield, which at the time was the centre of England's silk weaving industry.

2 Follow the path as it heads left and steadily up across the hillside,

WALK 8 – HOLLINSCLOUGH AND CHROME HILL

becoming a vehicle track beyond a house. After 1.4km you reach **Booth Farm** at the top.

3 Turn right to join the lane for a few paces, then go through a gate on the right and walk parallel to the lane. In the second field swing right, initially following a farm track, before veering left up and across the walled pasture above **Stoop Farm**. At the very top reach a path junction by a gate in the wall. In 2022 the final scenes of the last episode of the TV series *Peaky Blinders* were filmed overlooking Chrome Hill.

4 Don't go through the gate but instead turn right and walk alongside the wall through more fields. Follow this waymarked route as it turns down a steep grassy slope and then left to climb the **Chrome Hill** ridge. Follow this all the way to the top. Locals tend to pronounce 'Chrome' to rhyme with 'room' and it's believed to derive from an Old English word meaning bent or twisted.

Descending Chrome Hill, with Parkhouse Hill beyond

SHORT WALKS PEAK DISTRICT

To the south can be seen the attractive hilltop village of Longnor. Its unspoilt cobbled market square is overlooked by the original market hall and handsome former coaching inn, plus one of the best fish and chip shops in the Peak District.

5 From the summit walk down the broad, grassy slope on the far side to the lane at the bottom. Turn right, go over a cattle grid then go right again onto the driveway (a public right of way) of **Stannery Farm**.

6 Continue straight ahead and cross a footbridge. On the far side turn left and follow a public footpath around the edge of the field beside a brook until you reach the lane (or alternatively stay on the main track to join the lane).

7 Turn right and walk along the lane back into Hollinsclough. Between March and October the Chapel Tearooms at Hollinsclough are open at weekends and Bank Holidays, serving light breakfasts, lunches and cream teas.

Nearing the top of Chrome Hill

Parkhouse Hill provides an exciting extra challenge

➕ To lengthen
If you fancy bagging a second hill then walk up the steep grassy slope of Parkhouse Hill, immediately east of Chrome Hill. It's a lung-busting 1km (45min) there-and-back to reach its 360m high summit.

Walking through a tropical sea

Because of its rounded outline and serrated edges Chrome Hill is sometimes called the Dragon's Back, but these are not the scales of a giant monster or dinosaur. In fact, around 350 million years ago when the Peak District lay near the equator this was once a vast tropical lagoon. Chrome Hill is what's known as a knoll reef or 'mud mound' created from these warm shallow waters when particles of shellfish, coral and mud on the seabed were bound together by aquatic invertebrates and algae to form the distinctive limestone feature we see today.

The Greyhound Inn is home to a microbrewery

WALK 9
Warslow and Revidge

Time 1hr 45min
Distance 4.7km (2.9 miles)
Climb 105m

Explore the quieter side of the Peak District on this wildlife-rich hill walk

Start/finish	Greyhound Inn, Leek Road, Warslow
Locate	///whites.bloodshot.gong
Cafes/pubs	Pub at Warslow
Transport	Buses from Ashbourne and Buxton, Moorlands Connect bus
Parking	Roadside in Warslow (SK17 0JN)
Toilets	Next to Warslow Village Hall

Above the village of Warslow is a gentle hill known simply as Revidge. It's topped with heather and a clump of pine trees and its open aspect gives sweeping views over the surrounding countryside. Also, since it's off the main tourist path, it's generally very quiet and there's a good chance of seeing iconic moorland birds like curlews. Some of the slopes on the way up are rough underfoot and after wet weather they can be muddy and boggy in places.

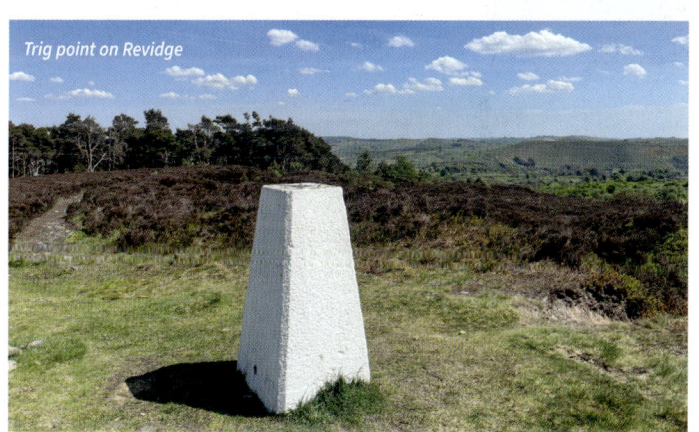
Trig point on Revidge

SHORT WALKS PEAK DISTRICT

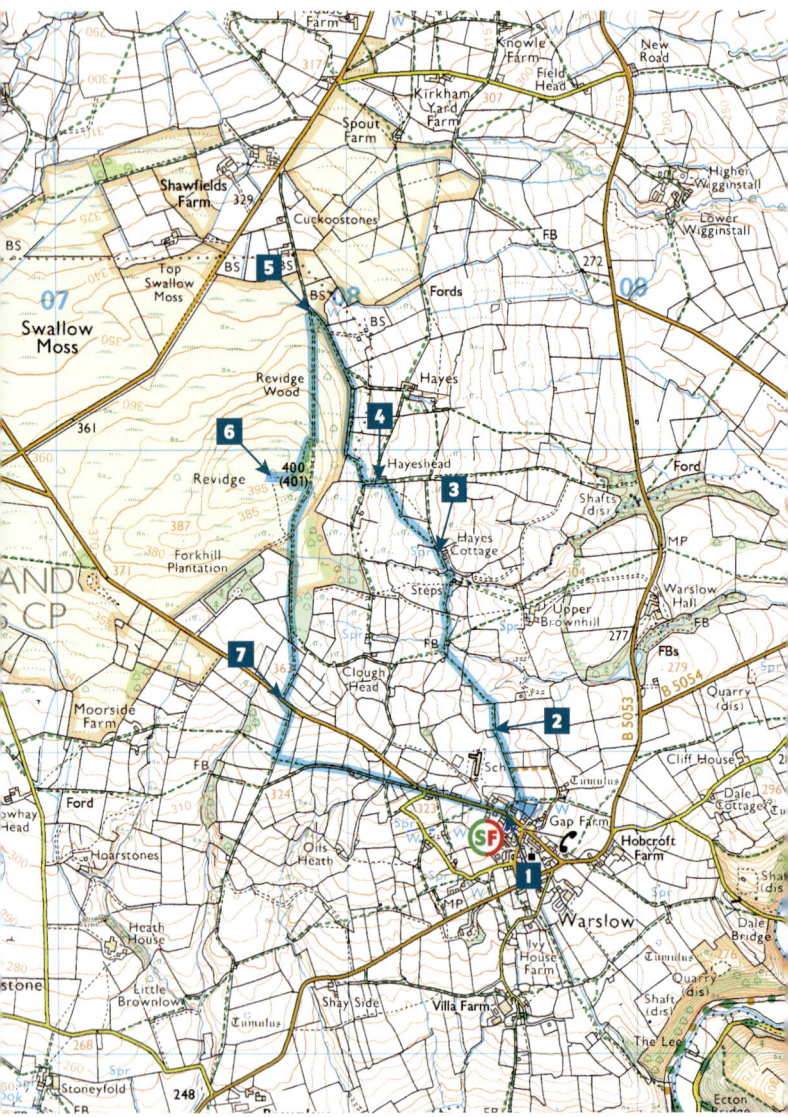

60

WALK 9 – WARSLOW AND REVIDGE

1 From the Greyhound Inn walk up Leek Road a few paces and turn right into Stacey Close. *The Greyhound Inn at Warslow has been serving thirsty travellers since 1750 and is now home to a microbrewery called Wilsons of Warslow.* Go right, through a paddock between buildings, then veer left following the waymarked route across fields next to a school until you get to the far corner of the school grounds.

2 Go ahead across the open field, then head half left across the undulating ground in the direction of the hilltop (Revidge). Keep right of a ruined barn, then swing right and follow the waymarked route across the fields to **Hayes Cottage**.

As you cross the fields look out for curlews, as well as the wheeling displays of black and white lapwings with their distinctive crests. In spring and summer skylarks are likely to be singing incessantly high overhead.

3 Pass the buildings on your right and at a signpost in the next field veer half left uphill to reach the deserted farm buildings of **Hayeshead**.

> ⓘ *Oatcakes are a Derbyshire and Staffordshire speciality, resembling soft pancakes and filled with savoury items like sausages, mushrooms and melted cheese.*

Deserted farm buildings at Hayeshead

The track to the top of Revidge

Traditional outbuildings like these were once used to store fodder, farm equipment and shelter animals in bad weather.

4 Continue straight up the hillside for another 50m, then turn right to follow a ditch gradually uphill. At the top turn right to walk alongside a wall then a farm drive for 500m until you reach a junction.

5 Turn sharply left and walk along the track across the ridge. As you approach the stand of pines at the top turn right for a narrow, stepped path that weaves its way through the heather to reach the trig point on **Revidge**. The name Revidge simply means 'rough edge' and there are expansive views in every direction from the 400m high summit.

6 Retrace your steps from the trig point for 75m and fork right to rejoin the summit track among the trees. Turn right and follow this broad route off the hilltop. Continue through a gate past woodland and ahead through a wall gap across the open hilltop and down to a road.

7 Cross over the road, turn left and almost immediately right off the road, and down through a field. Go left through a gate and cross the field to reach a track. Turn left and follow this back to **Warslow** and down the pavement to the start.

The call of the curlew

The curlew is Europe's largest wading bird and visits the Peak District moors each spring and summer to breed. With its long, curved beak and distinctive drawn-out bubbling call, the bird is unmistakable and closely associated with the Staffordshire moorlands. However, in recent years changes to their preferred nesting habitat (damp moorland and bog) caused by intensive farming, drainage and climate change, as well as predators and human disturbance, have caused their numbers to decline alarmingly and they are now a conservation priority species.

This walk is based on a route devised for 'Curlew Country', a two-year community project designed to raise awareness about the plight of the curlew through education and celebration, including school and community workshops and a sightings map.

A curlew in flight (photo: Phil Rhead)

Looking out of Thor's Cave

WALK 10
Wetton and Thor's Cave

Start/finish	*Wetton car park*
Locate	*///vitals.life.generally*
Cafes/pubs	*Cafe at Wetton Mill, pub at Wetton*
Transport	*Moorlands Connect bus*
Parking	*Wetton car park, Carr Lane, Wetton (DE6 2AF)*
Toilets	*At car park*

Time 2hr 30min
Distance 6.8km (4.2 miles)
Climb 230m

An energetic and adventurous walk to a spectacular cave high above the Manifold valley

There's drama aplenty on this exciting walk up to a large cave and airy viewpoint that tower above the River Manifold. A long descent then leads to an easy stretch along the leafy valley bottom, before a finish across open grassy hillsides with wide-ranging views. Warning: the open hilltop summit above the cave (which can be avoided by a shortcut) has precipitous and unfenced drops; and accessing the cave itself involves a short scramble up slippery rocks.

Thor's Cave seen from the Manifold Way

SHORT WALKS PEAK DISTRICT

WALK 10 – WETTON AND THOR'S CAVE

The approach path to Thor's Cave

1 Turn right out of the car park and walk along the lane to a junction. Go right and at the far end turn left. In a few paces branch left on a walled track signposted Thor's Cave. Follow this route across a field and up steps to a path junction.

2 Turn left for a short steep path to the top of the grassy pinnacle and viewpoint above Thor's Cave. Thor's Cave featured in the 1988 horror fantasy film *The Lair of the White Worm*, directed by Ken Russell and based on a short story by Bram Stoker.

3 Return to Waypoint 2 and at the path junction continue walking down the stepped path and around the hillside to the mouth of **Thor's Cave**.

> Thor's Cave is a natural cave system carved out by water thousands of years ago and located high in a steep limestone crag overlooking the valley. Animal and human remains dating back to the Bronze Age have been found here.

4 Follow the main path below the cave entrance down the wooded

Steps up to the cave entrance

hillside. When you reach a junction turn left onto a broader downhill path and at the bottom cross the river via a footbridge. Turn right onto the Manifold Way and follow this alongside the **River Manifold** for 0.7km until you reach a lane.

> The Manifold Way or Track is a 12km walking and cycling route that follows a former railway line from Hulme End to Waterhouses. It was acquired by Staffordshire County Council when the line closed in 1934 and became one of the country's first 'railway trails'.

5 Turn left and take the right of two parallel minor roads. At the end turn

Wetton Mill refreshments

right to cross the bridge to **Wetton Mill** (spelt Wettonmill on some maps). Formerly a water-powered corn mill, Wetton Mill now houses a popular National Trust tea room and holiday accommodation.

Because of the porous limestone bedrock, the River Manifold often disappears underground. It does so below Wetton Mill bridge via natural fissures known as swallets, only to reappear 8km later in Ilam Park (see Walk 13).

6 Walk past the front of the tea room and turn left between buildings on a footpath. Go uphill then at the top swing left and down into a dry valley, with **Wetton Hill** towering above. Turn left at the bottom and follow a broad grassy track for almost 1km until you reach a house.

7 Go through the gate at the end of the lane and turn right to cross the stream by a stone slab bridge. Climb the long sloping hillside ahead beside a wall on your right. At the top go through the gate ahead, over fields for a track into **Wetton** village. Turn left onto the road, go past the pub, and take the first right to return to the start.

> ⓘ *The world toe wrestling championships began at Ye Olde Royal Oak pub at Wetton in 1974 when some friends decided to invent a sport that the British could win!*

▬ To shorten

Omit the there-and-back detour to the open hilltop and viewpoint at Waypoint 2, saving 350m and 30m of steep ascent.

Exploring Thor's Cave

Thor's Cave has long been popular with visitors and it even had its own station on the valley's short-lived railway, handy in the 1920s when thousands came to watch druidical re-enactments performed at the cave by an eccentric preacher. The domed main cave is substantial and a torch may be useful to help explore its dark inner recesses, which are narrow and uneven. However, repeated bottom-sliding over the years has rendered some of the rock surfaces highly polished and as a result very slippery, so take care.

The Manifold Way leaving Hulme End

WALK 11
Hulme End and Ecton Hill

Start/finish	*Manifold Valley Visitor Centre, Hulme End*
Locate	*///masterful.plug.headlines*
Cafes/pubs	*Cafe by visitor centre, pub at Hulme End*
Transport	*Buses from Ashbourne and Buxton, Moorlands Connect bus*
Parking	*Manifold Valley Visitor Centre (SK17 0EZ)*
Toilets	*At visitor centre*

Time 2hr
Distance 5.7km (3.5 miles)
Climb 165m

A gentle hike to a panoramic hilltop once the centre of a valuable copper mining industry

Although lead mining was more common in the Peak District, a large grassy hill overlooking the Manifold valley was once prized for its rich veins of copper. This walk takes you steadily up to its open summit, from where there are wonderful views, followed by a long, grassy descent that may be slippery when wet. It begins and ends on the former trackbed of an unusual narrow-gauge railway line.

Manifold Valley Visitor Centre

Trig point on Ecton Hill summit

1 From the visitor centre at **Hulme End** walk along the **Manifold Way** down the valley. After 300m turn left on a signposted footpath over meadows via a boardwalk, then cross a footbridge over the river to reach **Westside Mill**.

Hulme End was the northern terminus of the Leek and Manifold Light Railway, a curious 13km-long narrow-gauge line that briefly ran in the early 1900s. The former station building is now a visitor centre and the engine shed a tea room.

2 Turn right and walk along the lane for 150m. At the bend turn left on to a drive, go right over a stile and then half left up across fields on a waymarked route. Pass to the right of a house and drop down through the next field to the bottom far corner. Turn left and walk along the lane for 150m to **East Ecton**.

3 Turn right up the driveway of Yew Tree Cottage and ahead at the bend to slant up left across hillside fields. At the lane turn right by a barn and in a few paces right again for a gently rising track. Follow this to the very far end of the track.

4 Go through the small wall gate, with what looks like a field barn just beyond. This stone building in fact once housed a steam engine used to

WALK 11 – HULME END AND ECTON HILL

haul the ore up from the mines far below. Follow the broad grassy path directly uphill beside a wall to the trig point on the top of **Ecton Hill**.

The hilltop is peppered with former shafts, since the copper ore was found in vertical 'pipes'.

One shaft is 550m deep, much of which is below the River Manifold, making it the deepest mine in Britain when it was sunk in the mid 1700s.

5 Continue ahead along the top of the slope past fenced-off shafts, with

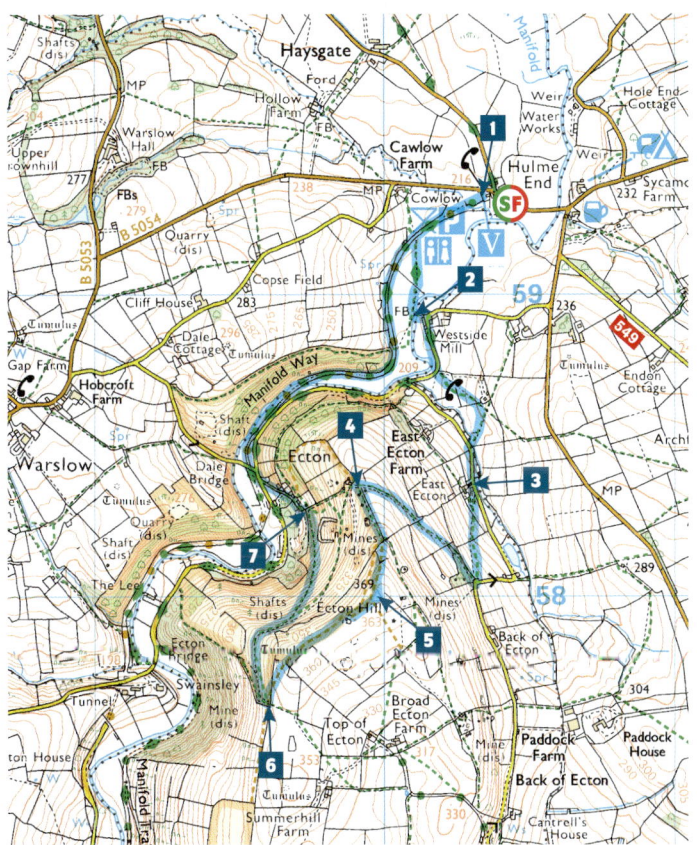

A capped and fenced mineshaft on the top of Ecton Hill

the Manifold valley below to your right, and on beside a wall. Go through a gate and drift half right down through a field to cross a gated stile in the wall.

6 Follow the path downhill past gorse bushes. In 130m look for an easily missed narrow grassy path on the right. Follow this around and down the wide grassy hillside, forking left to keep below a crescent of trees that masks a former spoil heap. At the very bottom you reach a stile by buildings. This is the site of the Geoff Cox Study Centre which promotes educational research into geology and mining.

In its brief heyday Ecton Copper Mine made the Duke of Devonshire a wealthy man and financed the building of Buxton's opulent Georgian townscape, including The Crescent (see Walk 6). The mine closed in 1889 and is now a Scheduled Monument.

7 Go over the stile and turn right, under the archway and past the copper-spired 'castle' or folly. Walk down the drive to the lane at the bottom. Turn right then immediately left at the junction. Take the Manifold Way on the right and follow this back to the start.

The copper-spired folly at the foot of Ecton Hill

▬ To shorten

At Waypoint 4 go straight ahead by the former mine engine house for a direct and steep path down the grassy hillside to reach Waypoint 7, saving 1.5km (45min) and 65m of ascent.

WALK 12
Hartington and Beresford Dale

Start/finish	Market Place, Hartington
Locate	///coasting.wicket.wisdom
Cafes/pubs	Cafes and pubs in Hartington
Transport	Buses from Ashbourne and Buxton, Moorlands Connect bus
Parking	Parsons Field car park, Hartington (SK17 0BE)
Toilets	Hartington

Time 1hr 45min
Distance 6.6km (4.1 miles)
Climb 140m

Follow gentle waterside paths and high field tracks around Hartington to discover the Dove's enduring charm

The Dove is one of the most picturesque rivers in the Peak District, nowhere more so than south of Hartington where it carves its way through the limestone hills. It's a favourite with anglers as well as walkers, immortalised long ago in a best-selling philosophical book on fishing. This easy route follows the river through a narrow, wooded dale, then via elevated walled tracks for superb views over both the Dove and Manifold valleys.

Hartington Cheese Shop specialises in locally made Blue Stilton

The popular path from Hartington to Beresford Dale

1 From the Market Place in the centre of Hartington walk along Warslow Road past the Charles Cotton pub and in 150m turn left for a public footpath next to the public toilets. Follow the well-walked path out across fields, over a walled lane and ahead through more undulating fields until you reach **Morson Wood**.

Large field barn near Hartington

2 Follow the route through the trees and down to join the River Dove, then on through the narrow rocky gorge of **Beresford Dale** over one footbridge until you reach a second. Cross to the far bank and continue downstream over a wide meadow until you reach another bridge at the entrance to Wolfscote Dale. Excavations of the cave high up in the rocks to the left uncovered human remains, decorative items and animal bones from the Romano British period.

3 Turn left before the gate and follow the track uphill away from the dale and river. At a crossroads of paths go straight on until you reach the lane at the very top. Turn left and walk along the lofty and seldom-used

WALK 12 – HARTINGTON AND BERESFORD DALE

lane for 1km until you reach a junction of routes on a tight bend. Looking north west there are great views over the wide Manifold valley to the high moors above Buxton and the Goyt valley.

4 Go right then immediately left up a gently rising walled track that soon levels out until you reach a junction.

5 Turn sharply left and walk along **Highfield Lane**, a broad unsurfaced walled track, across the hilltop for

1.3km. Drop down past a barn to reach a lane.

6 Turn left and follow the road down past the youth hostel and back to the centre of the **Hartington**. Hartington Hall is an imposing manor house built around 1600 and now a popular YHA youth hostel.

In 1203 Hartington became the first village in Derbyshire to be granted a market charter. Off the attractive main square is the well-stocked Cheese Shop, where you can pick up locally made specialities like Blue Stilton, Peakland White and Sage Derby.

> ⓘ *Derbyshire is one of only three English counties (alongside Leicestershire and Nottinghamshire) licensed to produce Blue Stilton cheese.*

Limestone cliffs and cave from the valley bottom path

Hartington Hall Youth Hostel is housed in a Jacobean manor house

— To shorten

At Waypoint 4 stay on the road at the sharp bend and follow this (Reynards Lane) all the way back to Hartington, saving 1km (30min) and 75m of ascent.

The philosophy of angling

The Compleat Angler was first published in 1653 and is ostensibly a practical guide to fly fishing. Author Izaak Walton based it on the experiences of fishing the Dove for trout and grayling with his friend Charles Cotton, who lived at Beresford Hall near Hartington. But 'The Contemplative Man's Recreation' (to give the book its full title) is more than simply a fishing manual. It includes narrative prose, excerpts of poetry and philosophical discourse on life as much as angling. Although the text may seem a little archaic today, at the time it was hugely popular, ran into numerous editions and has been reprinted many times.

Ilam Cross

WALK 13
Ilam and the Manifold valley

Time 2hr 45min
Distance 8.3km (5.2 miles)
Climb 215m

Start/finish	Ilam Hall
Locate	///headings.topical.thing
Cafes/pubs	Tea room at Ilam Hall
Transport	Moorlands Connect bus
Parking	National Trust Ilam Hall car park (DE6 2AZ)
Toilets	Ilam Hall

Discover an elegant hall and estate village on this long but uncomplicated walk around the lower Manifold valley

Tucked away in a deep fold of the Manifold valley, Ilam (pronounced 'eye lamb') is a fascinating place that includes the remnants of a stately hall, an Alpine-style estate village and a scenic network of paths. This long but scenic route heads up onto the ridge high above the valley for wonderful views, before a riverside return to Ilam. There's one steep climb up open hillside and a short section of country lane, otherwise it's straightforward and easy to follow.

Ilam Hall

SHORT WALKS PEAK DISTRICT

1 From the tea room at **Ilam Hall** walk down via the terraced garden and lawn to Holy Cross Church and turn right to reach **St Bertram's Bridge**. Bertram was an 8th-century local holy man and hermit whose tomb can be found inside the church. Don't cross the bridge but instead turn right to follow the riverside path for 1km until you reach a footbridge on the left.

At the foot of the rockface beside the path are so-called boil holes. Here the River Manifold, which in prolonged dry weather disappears underground below Wetton Mill, bubbles back up to the surface.

2 Go over the bridge, cross a field to a large solitary tree and then head half left for a path up the open hillside

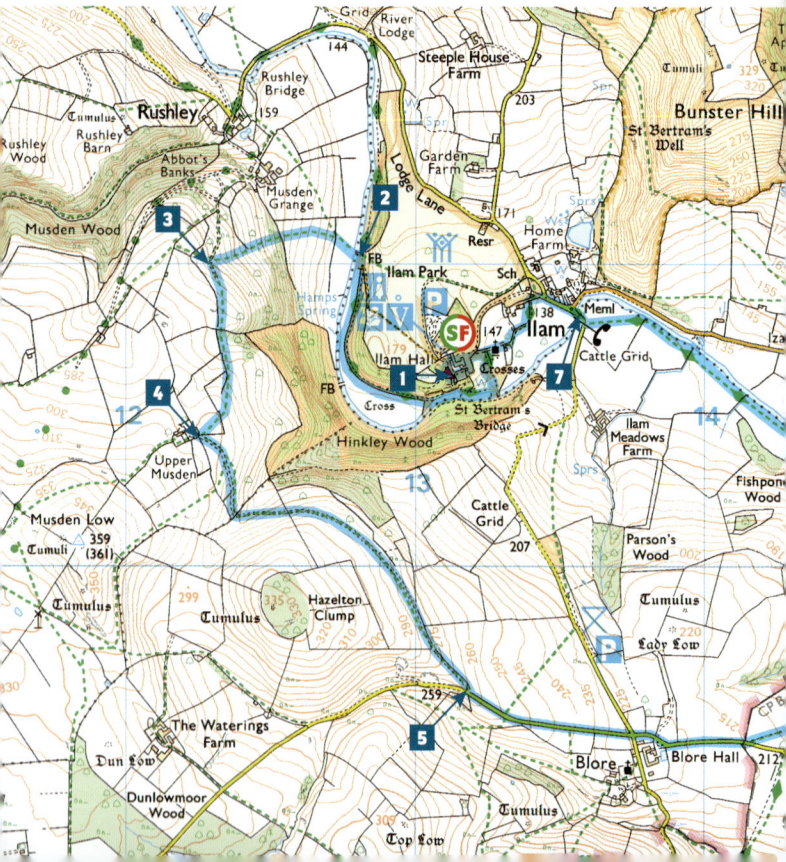

The River Manifold in Ilam Park

directly ahead. Continue climbing steeply through scrub until just before the top you reach a grassy cross-track.

3 Turn left and follow this route gently uphill and on beside a wall through hilltop fields. Just before the wall finishes go over a wall stile to cross a field to reach the ruins of **Upper Musden**.

4 Go sharp left, back out onto the open slope, and follow an obvious farm track across the slope ahead, below the wooded hill of **Hazelton Clump**. After 1.5km you reach a lane. There are terrific views across the valley to the mouth of Dove Dale, framed by the prominent peaks of Bunster Hill and Thorpe Cloud.

Looking towards Dove Dale from above Ilam

> ⓘ *The highest point in Staffordshire is Cheeks Hill, on Axe Edge Moor, at an elevation of 520m.*

5 Turn left and walk down the lane and over the crossroads by **Blore Hall**, then 450m beyond this go left over a stile and down a sloping field to the left of **Coldwall Farm**. Continue down a second field until just before **Coldwall Bridge**.

6 Don't cross the bridge and instead turn left and follow a path along the bottom of the slope through trees and scrub, then beside the river for over 1.5km until you reach the bridge at **Ilam**.

7 Cross the bridge and walk past Ilam Cross into the village.

Ilam Cross was built in 1841 by Ilam Hall's owner Jesse Watts-Russell as a tribute to his wife Mary. Its design was modelled on the famous Eleanor Crosses erected by Edward I in memory of his own wife after her death in 1290.

Turn left before the main vehicle entrance to Ilam Hall, then left again on a surfaced path by Dovedale House and follow this through **Ilam Park** back to the start.

Ilam Hall and estate village

What you see of Ilam Hall today are the remnants of a larger complex originally dating from the 1820s. A century later it was partly demolished by its then owner, flour manufacturer Robert McDougall, but what survived was gifted to the Youth Hostel Association and National Trust. Today it's a popular place to stay and visit, with the terraced garden and courtyards giving a hint of a much grander past.

Meanwhile Ilam's picturesque setting inspired an earlier owner to commission architect Sir George Gilbert Scott to rebuild the original estate buildings in an Alpine or 'cottage orné' Swiss chalet style that was popular during the Romantic movement.

Ilam's rustic-style estate village

Viator's Bridge

WALK 14
Milldale and the River Dove

Time 1hr 30min
Distance 4.5km (2.8 miles)
Climb 155m

Enjoy the wildlife and natural beauty of the limestone dales on this up and down circuit around Milldale

Start/finish	National Trust's Milldale Information Point
Locate	///suave.neon.laminate
Cafes/pubs	Seasonal kiosk at Milldale
Transport	Moorlands Connect bus
Parking	Milldale car park (DE6 2GB)
Toilets	By bridge at start

The unspoilt hamlet of Milldale sits on the River Dove near Alstonefield, hidden away deep in the narrow leafy valley. It's a tranquil setting and this short route explores the lovely riverside, framed by rocky crags and rich in birdlife, then climbs the wooded hillside to appreciate the spectacle from above. The ascent of Nabs Dale is a little rocky underfoot and watch out for nettles in high summer, but the reward is a peaceful and scenic route away from the crowds.

Rolling fields above the dale

SHORT WALKS PEAK DISTRICT

1 At Milldale cross **Viator's Bridge** and turn right to follow the wide riverside path. Viator's Bridge is a small and narrow packhorse bridge made famous in Izaak Walton's book *The Compleat Angler*. The dale becomes more wooded and after 1.2km you reach a path junction in a clearing.

As you walk along the riverside look out for dippers, an iconic bird of the Peak District often seen bobbing up and down on rocks mid-stream. With its dark brown plumage and distinctive white bib, it's also an agile underwater swimmer.

2 Turn left for the path signposted Alsop-en-le-Dale. Follow this narrow and in places rocky route all the way to the very top of Nabs Dale.

3 Go up and into the field ahead, turning half left at the signpost to follow a route across fields above (but not through or beside) **Hanson Grange**. This historic dwelling was once a monastic sheep farm (known as a grange) and was owned by the monks of Burton Abbey. Turn right and join a track past a building called **Nabs View** to reach a crossroads of routes.

The gentle path beside the River Dove

4 Turn half left for a public footpath (unsignposted) diagonally across the open hilltop field, aiming for the upper far corner. Go through the wall gap and keeping the same line drop down across four more fields, aiming just to the right of a field barn, until you reach the top edge of the dale with spectacular views across the valley.

5 Turn left and follow the path along the top of the slope, past **Shining Tor**, with the river far below to your right. When you come to a wall go over the stile and ahead down a slope. Follow the steeply winding path all the way back down to **Milldale**.

Limestone cliffs south of Milldale

Although long gone, a small water-powered mill known as Ochre Mill once stood beside the river at this location and was used to produce red and yellow ochre powder, which was a key ingredient in the making of lead paint.

> **– To shorten**
>
> At Waypoint 4 turn sharply left for the path signposted Milldale that descends directly through fields back to the start, saving 500m or 15min.

A wilder River Dove

To make the Dove attractive for angling the river was once artificially stocked with fish and over 170 small weirs were built to create artificial pools and trap fish. But now some weirs have been dismantled so that the fish can spawn naturally and only the native (and unstocked) brown trout remain. Returning the river to a wilder state also benefits wildlife, including invertebrates and insects vital for a healthy river ecosystem. Further downstream, near Uttoxeter, the open riverside has been planted with hundreds of trees to provide shade and prevent erosion and so help the Dove's recovering salmon population.

WALK 15
Dove Dale

Start/finish	*National Trust Dove Dale car park*
Locate	*///hoops.continues.shortage*
Cafes/pubs	*Seasonal kiosk at car park*
Transport	*Moorlands Connect bus*
Parking	*National Trust Dove Dale car park, Thorpe Road (DE6 2AY)*
Toilets	*At car park*

Time 2hr 45min
Distance 7.5km (4.7 miles)
Climb 240m

Scale the heights and step across the water on this adventurous exploration of dramatic Dove Dale

There are few places in the Peak District more famous – and justifiably so – than the lower section of Dove Dale, with the gurgling river framed by dramatic limestone cliffs, plunging woodland and some very photogenic stepping stones. This varied route with spectacular viewpoints aplenty explores the dale from top to bottom, combining a few steep slopes and rough paths with easy riverside stretches, but time your visit carefully to avoid crowds at peak times.

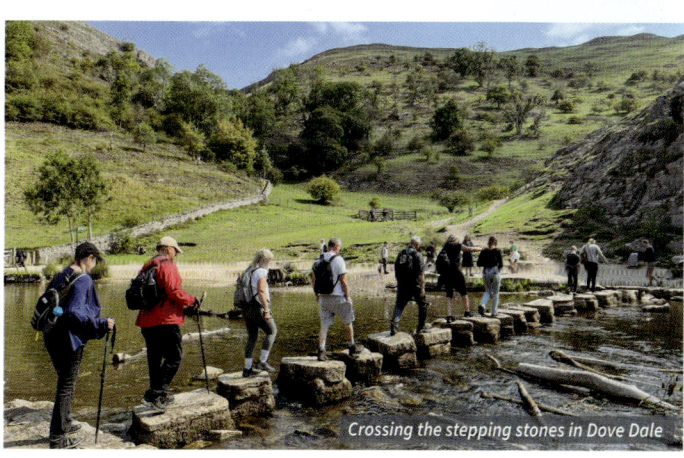
Crossing the stepping stones in Dove Dale

SHORT WALKS PEAK DISTRICT

1 From the car park walk down the main track towards Dove Dale. In the 1930s there was a campaign to make Dove Dale its own national park, before the entire Peak District was eventually designated in 1951. At the water gauging station turn left for a gated path signposted as an alternative route to Ilam. Go up the steps and follow this path beside the wall for 850m.

2 Turn right at a sign to 'viewpoint' for a path up to the ridge top, then swing right and continue across and gently down the slope below **Bunster Hill**. At a wall turn right and head up the long hillside until you reach a gate on the left just before the top. Go through this and head diagonally right across the field to a wide, walled lane.

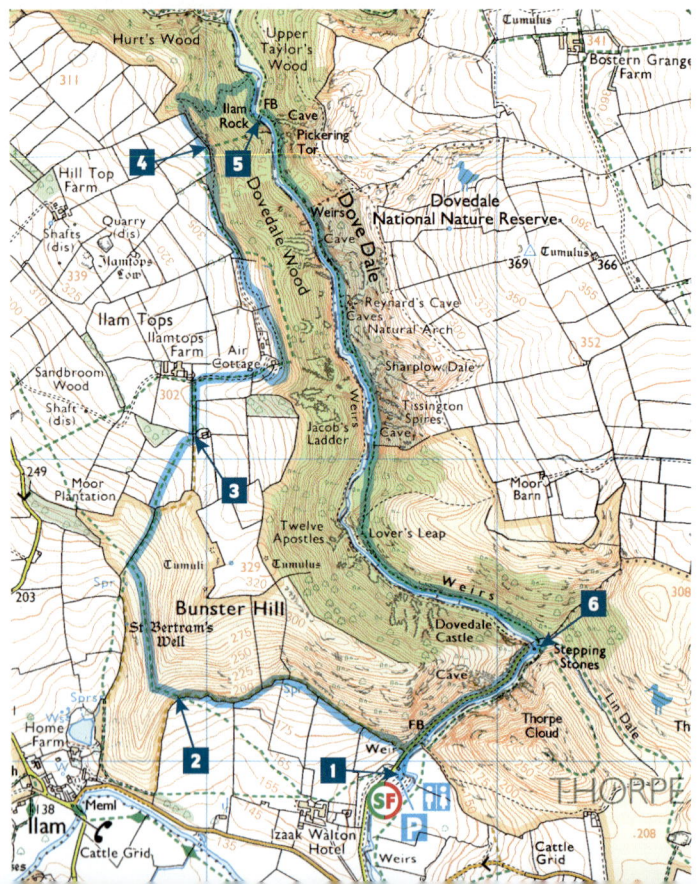

WALK 15 – DOVE DALE

3 Turn left to **Ilamtops Farm**, then right as far as **Air Cottage**. Go right, down a short open slope, then swing left on a clearly waymarked route across the rocky and part-wooded hillside below Air Cottage. Veer right across an open slope to enter **Dovedale Wood** and follow the path to a second junction.

Ash dieback has devastated parts of Dove Dale's native woodland, threatening important wildlife habitats, but an ambitious project is now restoring the precious valley woodland at the heart of the national nature reserve, see www.lifeintheravines.co.uk.

4 Turn left, indicated as 'Alternative route via steps', for a gently winding path down the wooded hillside (the public footpath to the right is a steep and difficult scramble). At the junction at the bottom turn right to cross the footbridge below **Ilam Rock**.

Among Dove Dale's spectacular landforms are huge limestone pinnacles such as Ilam Rock and the Twelve Apostles, plunging screes and sheer rockfaces with numerous caves, as well as Thorpe Cloud and Bunster Hill that tower over the mouth of the dale.

Ilam Rock

5 Turn right and follow the riverside path through **Dove Dale** for 2km to reach the stepping stones. The rocky promontory of Lover's Leap passed on the way is where a woman's tragic fall was supposedly averted when her billowing skirt caught on branches.

6 Cross the **stepping stones** and turn left along the track back to the start, or follow the rough path along the south east bank to cross lower down by the footbridge if you prefer. For almost its entire length the River Dove forms the county border between Staffordshire (west bank) and Derbyshire (east bank).

Thorpe Cloud with the stepping stones at its foot

✚ To lengthen

To finish with the energetic ascent of Thorpe Cloud turn left at the stepping stones (Waypoint 6) and follow the waymarked path along Lin Dale to climb the hill from behind, then continue on the same route around the lower slope and cross a footbridge near the car park. This is a walk of around 2km (1hr) with 140m of ascent.

Stepping stones across the Dove

Dove Dale has been a tourist hotspot since Victorian times when the famous stepping stones connecting Derbyshire to Staffordshire were first laid. In 2024 they were repaired after debris washed down the river during Storm Babet dislodged several of the 16 limestone-capped boulders. Take care when using them after rain, since the river level can rise significantly and the stones may be slippery. Also be aware that there may be queues to cross at busy times, but generally if you visit in the morning or on a weekday rather than weekend or Bank Holiday you can still enjoy this beautiful location in peace.

USEFUL INFORMATION

Tourism bodies

Visit Peak District & Derbyshire
www.visitpeakdistrict.com

Peak District National Park
www.peakdistrict.gov.uk

National Trust
www.nationaltrust.org.uk

Visit Buxton
www.visitbuxton.co.uk

Tourist information centres

Buxton Visitor Centre,
The Pump Room, The Crescent
https://buxtoncrescentexperience.com/plan-your-visit-2

Buses

Bus from Buxton, Whaley Bridge and New Mills
www.highpeakbuses.com

Buses from Buxton and Sheffield
www.stagecoachbus.com

On-demand (pre-booked) minibus service across the Staffordshire Moorlands
www.moorlandsconnect.co.uk

Trains

Trains to Buxton from Manchester
www.northernrailway.co.uk

The River Dove near the end of Walk 15

© Andrew McCloy 2026
First edition 2026
ISBN: 978 1 78631 259 4
eISBN: 978 1 78765 255 2

Printed in Singapore by KHL Printing using responsibly sourced paper.
A catalogue record for this book is available from the British Library.
All photographs are by the author unless otherwise stated.

© Crown copyright and database rights 2026 OS AC0000810376

Cicerone's EU representative for GPSR compliance is Easy Access System Europe, Mustamäe tee 50, 10621 Tallinn, Estonia. Email gpsr.requests@easproject.com.

CICERONE

Cicerone Press, Juniper House, Murley Moss, Oxenholme Road,
Kendal, Cumbria, LA9 7RL

www.cicerone.co.uk

Updates to this Guide

While every effort is made to ensure the accuracy of guidebooks as they go to print, changes can occur during the lifetime of an edition. Any updates that we know of for this guide will be on the Cicerone website (www.cicerone.co.uk/1259/updates), so please check before planning your trip. We also advise that you check information about transport, accommodation and shops locally. Even rights of way can be altered over time. We are always grateful for information about any discrepancies between a guidebook and the facts on the ground, sent by email to updates@cicerone.co.uk.

Register your book: To sign up to receive free updates, special offers and GPX files where available, create a Cicerone account and register your purchase via the 'My Account' tab at www.cicerone.co.uk.